THE VOICE *of* RADIANCE

-a luminous journey of heart, soul and nature's light

POETRY

Mamazzad Ahmed Choudhury
(Babu)

Composition period of the poem: 1986-96

First Edition: 2025
Paperback Published by Pothi in India and Globally via Amazon Kindle Direct Publishing (KDP), Lulu & Draft2Digital.

ISBN (Paperback): 978-93-343-9632-4
ISBN (eBook): 978-93-343-8210-5

Distribution & Availability Rights:

"The Voice of Radiance" is published under the full and independent distribution rights of the poet.

The paperback edition, carrying the author's official ISBN, is available in India via Amazon.in, Flipkart, Pothi Store, and internationally through Lulu Bookstore & major Amazon marketplaces including the US, UK, NL, Germany, France, Italy, Spain, Japan, Canada, Australia, Poland, Sweden, Brazil, and Mexico.

The eBook edition is published under the author's ownership & is available globally on platforms such as Amazon Kindle Store, Google Play Books, Apple Books & other supported e-reading platforms.

Both editions are catalogued using the author's own ISBNs and are eligible for acquisition by:
•Libraries and educational institutions
•Academic retailers and bookstores
•Digital and print distribution networks

For rights, licensing, or distribution inquiries, please contact: **mamazzad.choudhury123@gmail.com**

Preface

Poetry, at its finest, is both mirror and window - reflecting the soul of the poet while opening vistas into the human condition. This volume, composed by **Mamazzad Ahmed Choudhury (Babu Choudhury),** *is a testament to that dual nature. Rooted in lived experience and elevated by a lyrical sensibility, the collection traverses landscapes both intimate and vast - emotional terrains marked by longing, resilience, beauty, and quiet introspection.*

Drawing from a rich cultural heritage and deep engagement with language, Choudhury's verse carries echoes of Sufi spirituality, Bengali romanticism, and modernist reflection, yet remains unmistakably his own. Whether evoking a solitary walk under rain-laden skies or capturing the flicker of hope in the eyes of the displaced, these poems resonate with empathy and finely wrought emotional clarity.

Language here serves as both vessel and voyage. Nature, loss, belonging, and the metaphysical - each finds a place within these pages, not as isolated themes but as interwoven strands of a poet's evolving consciousness.

This collection is not only a personal offering but a cultural document - situated at the confluence of history, identity, and poetic form. It speaks to readers from all walks of life, yet remains deeply grounded in the specificity of the poet's experience, shaped by geography, ancestry, and imagination.

In these poems, **Mamazzad Ahmed Choudhury** *invites us into his inner world - not for the sake of mere confession, but to create a shared space where thought and feeling find resonance.*

Acknowledgments

The creation of "**THE VOICE *of* RADIANCE**" - has been a journey of devotion, reflection, and learning. I am deeply indebted to many individuals and institutions whose guidance, support, and inspiration have made this work possible.

First and foremost, I bow in gratitude to the Almighty, the source of wisdom and light, without whose grace no word could have taken shape.

I express my heartfelt thanks to my family, whose encouragement, patience, and love have been my constant strength. Their silent sacrifices allowed me the time and space to compose and refine these poems.

My deep appreciation extends to my students and colleagues, who constantly reminded me of the true purpose of education: to inspire, uplift, and enlighten. Their youthful curiosity has shaped the pedagogical design of this Edition.

I also acknowledge the timeless voices of poets and thinkers - past and present - whose works continue to guide humanity. Their words resonate like eternal torches, reminding us of our shared duty to truth and beauty.

Finally, I offer gratitude to all poetry lovers, educators, and institutions across the world who will engage with this collection. It is my hope that "**THE VOICE *of* RADIANCE**" will become not just a book of poems, but a companion in classrooms, libraries, and hearts worldwide.

Mamazzad Ahmed Choudhury (Babu)
Poet & Educator

Dedication

To all seekers of light, knowledge, and truth-
May these humble verses inspire young minds,
comfort weary hearts, and awaken in every reader
the eternal flame of wisdom.

Invocation

O words, take wings of light,
Carry truth through darkest night.
In every heart, let wisdom grow,
In every soul, let radiance flow.

O verses, bloom like morning flower,
Awaken love with gentle power.
May nations hear your tender call,
A song of peace uniting all.

O book, be torch for minds to see,
A path of hope, eternally.
Let seekers find in every line,
The Voice of Radiance - pure, divine.

TABLE OF CONTENTS

Poetry: Origins, Evolution and Essence

Poetry (from the Greek poiesis, meaning "making") is a form of literary art that employs aesthetic and often rhythmic qualities of language to evoke meanings that extend beyond, or even replace, literal expression. Any particular instance of poetry is called a poem and is created by a poet. To achieve artistic effects, poets employ a wide range of techniques known as poetic devices, including assonance, alliteration, consonance, euphony and cacophony, onomatopoeia, rhythm, rhyme schemes, and sound symbolism.

Most written poems are structured in verse - a sequence or arrangement of lines that follow a particular poetic form. Consequently, the term verse has also become synonymous with poetry itself.

Many poetic traditions are deeply rooted in specific cultures and languages. Readers familiar with Dante, Goethe, Mickiewicz, or Rumi may associate poetry primarily with rhyme and regular meter. However, other traditions employ different methods of creating rhythm and euphony: Biblical poetry and Old English alliterative verse, for example, rely less on rhyme, while Somali poetry is built on intricate systems of alliteration and metre that function independently of writing, comparable in structure to ancient Greek and medieval European oral traditions.

Much of modern poetry challenges earlier conventions - sometimes testing the principle of euphony, sometimes abandoning rhyme and fixed rhythm altogether.

Poetry often relies on forms and conventions that allow words to carry multiple layers of interpretation, frequently evoking strong emotional responses. Ambiguity, symbolism, irony, and other stylistic choices of poetic diction leave poems open to diverse readings. Figures of speech - such as metaphor, simile, and metonymy - create resonance between seemingly unrelated images, forging connections that may otherwise go unnoticed. This resonance can also arise between verses themselves, shaped by recurring patterns of rhyme, rhythm, or thematic echo.

The history of poetry is long and varied, evolving across cultures throughout the world. Its origins reach back to prehistoric times, with hunting poetry in Africa and panegyric or elegiac court poetry in the empires of the Nile, Niger, and Volta valleys. Some of the earliest known African written poetry appears in the Pyramid Texts of the 25th century BCE.

In Western Asia, the Epic of Gilgamesh, composed in Sumerian, is the earliest surviving epic poem. Elsewhere, early poetry includes folk songs such as the Chinese Shijing; sacred hymns such as the Sanskrit Rigveda, the Zoroastrian Gathas, the Hurrian songs, and the Hebrew Psalms; as well as epic retellings of oral traditions, including the Egyptian Story of Sinuhe, Indian epics, and Homer's Iliad and Odyssey.

Poetry: Mirror of the Soul, Flame of the Spirit

Poetry is the language of the soul, a reflection of human emotions, experiences, and imagination. Words, rhythm, and metaphors come together to create a bridge between the inner world and the universe around us. Over the years - through my childhood, professional journey as an educator, and observations of society - I have gathered experiences and reflections that have gradually taken the form of poems.

This collection, "THE VOICE *of* RADIANCE"*- a luminous journey of heart, soul and nature's light is the culmination of that lifelong journey. It covers a wide range of themes: nature, human relationships, society, patriotism, emotions, and spiritual reflections. Each poem is a window, inviting readers to explore their own thoughts, memories, and emotions while connecting with universal human experiences. I believe poetry is not only a form of literature but also an instrument of learning, moral reflection, and social awareness.*

I extend my heartfelt gratitude to all who encouraged and supported this endeavor - my family, colleagues, students, and well-wishers. Above all, my country, its people, and the richness of its culture have been the greatest inspiration behind this collection. *It is my hope that this anthology will nourish the mind, stir the imagination, and illuminate the human spirit of every reader.*

"Where language ends, poetry begins - the infinite within the finite."

Poetry - Its Necessity, Reflection, and Eternal Whisper

Poetry is not merely written - it is breathed. It is the pulse of language, the whisper of the soul, the fire that keeps memory alive. Where prose explains, poetry reveals; where speech ends, poetry begins. In a handful of words, it can cradle an ocean of emotion, carrying grief without bitterness, joy without excess, and love without measure.

Its necessity lies in its power to rescue the unspoken - to give form to what trembles in the heart yet escapes the tongue. It preserves the fragrance of vanished moments, the voices of distant generations, the truth of a time that history may forget. Without poetry, language would have breadth but no depth; life would have motion but no music.

Yet poetry is not only a vessel; it is also a mirror. It reflects the poet's inner world and the world beyond the poet, revealing beauty and brokenness with equal grace. In its lines, we see ourselves as we are and as we dream to be. It is the intimate diary of the human spirit, yet shared with all humanity.

Poetry also begins where language meets wonder. It is the bridge between what we can say and what we can only feel. In its truest form, it is not a luxury of the mind, but a necessity of the soul - as essential as air, yet far rarer to find. Philosophers seek truth through reason; poets find it in the quiet spaces reason cannot enter. A single image, a sudden turn of phrase, can open a door that a thousand explanations could never unlock.

Its endurance is older than history, older than ink, older even than the alphabet. It began as a rhythm in the human breath, a chant by the fire, a cry to the heavens - and it has never ceased to speak. At its highest form, poetry is not simply language arranged with beauty; it is thought distilled to essence, feeling rendered into music. Each line is both mirror and lamp: a mirror in which the reader sees the truth of their own soul, and a lamp that casts light upon what they did not yet know they sought.

Poetry is both mirror and flame. In one breath, it shows us as we are; in the next, it lights the path to who we might become. It gathers sorrow without letting it decay into despair, and cradles joy without letting it fade into forgetfulness. It is the only art that can hold both a tear and a star in the same hand.

And so poetry endures - not as an ornament of language, but as its purest form; not as a relic of the past, but as a living breath in the present. It is the eternal whisper that follows us through the corridors of time, reminding us that while all things pass, the song of the human spirit remains.

"Poetry is the breath between heartbeats - unseen, yet it keeps the soul alive. It is where truth hides in beauty, and beauty hides the truth."

- Mamazzad Ahmed Choudhury (Babu)

Humanity

Feed the hungry, give drink to the dry,
Lift the fallen when they cannot try.
Break the chains where the captives weep,
Cradle the grieving in mercy deep.

Wound not a soul - let kindness be sown,
Give of yourself, fill nothing's your own.
For in such love, pure and free,
Dwells the heart of humanity.

Speak not harshly, let anger fade,
Stand for the voiceless, unafraid.
Reach across borders, stretch out your hand,
Plant seeds of hope across every land.

Heal the wounded, comfort the lost,
Carry the burden, no matter the cost.
Let laughter rise where sorrow has lain,
Transform the tears into gentle rain.

Cherish the stranger, embrace the weak,
In every language, let compassion speak.
For we are but threads in one grand weave,
Bound by the love we dare to believe.

The Lost Heart (Sonnet Form)

My heart was stolen when I did not see,
A fleeting glance unchained its secret song;
What once was mine now lives inside of thee,
Where all my restless dreams to thee belong.

I never thought such fate would bind my days,
Nor did I guess thy voice could rule my soul;
Yet in thine eyes I found a tender blaze,
A fire of love that makes my spirit whole.

I dreamt of skies where golden visions fly,
Of wings that soared beyond the reach of pain;
But thou hast caught me ‘neath thy gentle sky,
And bound me fast with love’s eternal chain.

So here I stand, no wish to flee apart -
For thou, my love, dost hold my captive heart.

The Beyond

The chariot waits, its reins slack in the stillness,
as if poised between departure and dream.
A summons drifts from the far-off steps of the
unknown, yet the ticket remains unstamped
on the brow of fate.

The final packing lies untouched -
Time, it seems, has not spoken the last word.
The lamp quivers in its own small universe,
its wavering flame whispering the music of partings.

I have heard -
beyond this shore lie a hundred jetties,
each one a riddle the river asks,
and only the traveler who braves the current
finds the language of light.

Breath gathers like a rising tide;
my eyes fall upon the quiet doormat by the door.
Who comes there -
a guest, or a silent envoy?

Perhaps Time itself stands waiting
to lower the veil on the bridal chamber of days.
We are all brief tenants of this bright inn,
guests of two sunrises at most.

When the festival of light is spent,
we go -
to the Beyond,
where no farewells are spoken,
and the horizon waits,
patient as eternity.

Youth

Youth is the dawn, a radiant flame,
A boundless sky where dreams proclaim.
It roars like thunder, fierce and strong,
A timeless fire, a marching song.

Youth is the storm of questions bold,
The courage to seek, the strength to unfold.
It shatters chains of false and wrong,
And lights the path where truths belong.

Not fleeting power, nor passing fire,
But the forge of nations, rising higher.
The youth of today, the guides of tomorrow,
Builders of hope from pain and sorrow.

Youth is the voice of a fearless creed,
The language of vision, the strength to lead.
It seeks horizons yet unknown,
And shapes a world to call its own.

Ode to Spring

O charming Spring, you knock upon my door,
As though my golden hour-knock, knock, knock-
I have seen eighteen seasons pass my life,
Yet none has touched me like today's Spring.

O Spring, O Spring, O lovely sovereign,
You are the king of all the circling seasons.

When Spring arrives, the pulse begins to stir,
The blood flows faster, quickened by your song.
The heart awakens, beating strong and clear,
Rising higher, lifted by your breath.

When Spring arrives, the spirit sprouts new leaves,
The skin recalls the thrill of sudden breeze,
And in the mind, a trembling joy takes wing,
A quiet awe, a state of pure renewal.

And when you linger, skies turn bright and wide,
Blossoms weave garlands on the earth's fair brow.
In every soul, a dream of hope takes root-
Promise of life, reborn through you, O Spring.

The Pedagogue

A teacher is the radiant flame,
A timeless guide, beyond all fame.
Through gentle care and steadfast hand,
They shape the future of every land.

Not merely a giver of lessons or art,
But a sculptor of character, a molder of heart.
They plant the seeds of truth and grace,
And nurture courage in every place.

No crown they wear, no throne they claim,
Yet nations rise upon their name.
In silent sacrifice, their greatness lies,
Their light enduring, their spirit wise.

A teacher is the morning star,
Illuminating paths from near to far.
Through every act, through word and deed,
They build the world each child will lead.

Rhythms of the Sky

The stars gather like children in playful chatter,
Twinkling secrets across the night's vast court.
Comets rush in haste, as messengers on errands,
Planets keep their paces, steadfast in their rounds.
Thus the universe breathes-
Order in seeming chaos, music in endless silence.

The moon hides in the lap of clouds,
While the clouds drift, carrying it close to their bosom.
Like a bashful bride, the veiled moon
Retreats to her inner chamber
At the arrival of the sun,
As though it were the rhythm of the sky's own
household.

The transit of Venus across the sun-
A rare and wondrous cosmic marvel.
When the moon stands between the earth and the sun,
It becomes that very solar eclipse.
It is the tale of a vast household-
Of joy and sorrow, clash and collision, inner strife.

Orbits, revolutions, positions, shifts of place-
All within fixed laws,
All in the measured cycle of time.

Allama Bishkuti :
The Eternal Voyager of Light

When humanity grew weary in the dark,
you lit the lamp of Truth.
Allama Bishkuti, you taught us-
love is the supreme language of life,
and compassion the true peace of the soul.

Your gathering was a haven of equality,
where rich and poor drank from the same stream.
You proclaimed-
there is no division among humankind,
for in the light of Truth, all stand as one.

My poetry is but a humble attempt
to hold your radiance in words.
If these verses awaken in the reader
a song of truth, compassion, and love,
then this journey of devotion finds its fulfillment.

First Love

I know you won't come,
yet my heart refuses to accept it.

I never betrayed you,
Never played with your life like a game.

You left, taking all the affection with you,
Leaving behind some sorrow, some memories.
Like a desolate bird wandering without purpose,
Your indifferent behavior bore not a trace of feeling.

I did not complain, I did not write a tale of grief -
This is but fate's cruel irony.

We once walked together by the shores of Sevan,
Never imagined life would bring such confusion.
What was to happen, has already passed -
Then why hold on to empty resentment?

On the journey of life, many come and go,
Some cry, and others smile as they flow.

Life

Flowing down from the hills into cascading streams,
Through vast lakes, rivers, and the soil's seams -
I dissolved into the sea, the ocean, the endless deep;
From where did I come, to where do I go,
So much clings to me as I flow.

So many have lifted me upon their path,
So many poured their thoughts, their wrath;
I accepted it all with a tranquil heart,
Not questioning, not tearing apart.

To many I gave life, from many I took it away.
But is that my fault ?
Why do they bathe in me with delight,
Why am I their joy, their rite ?

They built bridges across my chest,
Mechanical beasts now roam without rest.
They've narrowed my journey, confined my spread,
Turned my flowing lap into farmland instead.

Why do they trouble me so ?
Can I not resist, say no?

They've named me Life -
Painted me in colors, rejoiced in strife.
Across seven seas, through thirteen rivers I run,
After countless trials, I return where I begun.

Abode

You are the admirer of all that is beautiful and true,
You are the cherished abode of my life.
Behind every mastery I hold in life,
Flows the endless stream of your radiant spirit-
I have found illumination, even when forsaken by loved ones.

All have misunderstood me, but never you;
In your boundless love, I found new life anew.
You are the beloved and graceful one; you are my elixir,
In your free and lofty thoughts, my vessel has found its shore.

You are the dawn that breaks my darkest night,
The gentle hand that lifts me to the light.
Through storm and silence, your whisper I hear,
A song of solace, ever constant, ever near.

In your embrace, the world dissolves away,
And hope awakens with each breaking day.
No treasure or triumph could ever replace,
The boundless refuge I find in your grace.

Borderline

You are the sea, I am the river -
Crossing a hundred winding paths, I will merge into
you.

You are the sky, I am the bird -
Flying across a thousand leagues,
I will meet you at your borderline.

In my life, you are the saline drip,
The solution to countless problems.
In your presence, the battle has ceased; with your touch,
I have become immortal.

You have witnessed life by giving life,
And I live on through your glory.
I gaze into the distance - as far as the eye can see.
The sandy, desolate field - it feels like a desert.

Phrontistery

An educational institution is a beacon of light,
A sanctuary of wisdom, radiant and bright.
It opens the mind to horizons wide,
Where truth and knowledge gently abide.

Within its walls, new visions arise,
Hearts are inspired, and spirits grow wise.
In the bond of teacher and eager youth,
Flows the timeless river of learning and truth.

It is not mere lessons in books and art,
But a shaping ground of character and heart.
Here are nurtured values, discipline, and care,
The essence of humanity taught with prayer.

An institution stands as society's soul,
Guiding each generation toward its goal.
A foundation of progress, noble and grand,
The torchbearer of hope in every land.

Mirage

I have no address of my own,
I do not seek any dwelling or destination.
I am a wanderer, I am indifferent -
Perhaps I may drift away to distant China.

I am alive, I am spirited,
I am mortal, I am soaring.
I am a mirage, I am Fujiyama,
I am an island flame, I am Panama.

No home, no place, no bound I claim,
No walls to hold, no roof to name.
A drifting soul, the wind's own kin,
Perhaps I'll sail to far-off Qin.

I breathe, I burn, I laugh, I fly,
A mortal spark beneath the sky.
I am the shimmer, the Fujiyama flame,
An island's torch, Panama's name.

Endangered

India - my beloved land,
Today your every strand lies in peril.
Freedom unbound, privileges unchecked -
Too often are twisted to serve the abuse of power.

Corruption runs wild;
Looting, grand scandals without end -
Nothing remains undone,
All woven in the collusion of officials and politicians.

We heed no call
To discipline, to decency, to the rhythm of time.

Give us but ten years under steadfast rule,
And the spine of the nation will stand straight once more.
Every masked pretender will be unmasked,
And we shall be made whole - in body and in mind,
In thought, in conscience, in will, in spirit.

Nature's Lament

O Sun, O planets, O stars,
O sky, O air, O sea, O streams -
Nature has given us countless gifts,
In return, how much have we repaid?

On paper we have done much afforestation,
But in reality - nothing, only saffron-tinted decoration.
The oxygen in the air has dwindled,
While other elements have increased.
Instead of plants, we foolishly seek other solutions.

From eating adulterated food, the liver has grown weak,
The good is no longer digested, the bad overwhelms.
Guest birds no longer wish to come -
Owing to human behavior.
Tourists avoid the forests -
For the misdeeds of militants.

The Lamp of Learning

Education is no mere flame of books,
Nor lines of ink on silent pages kept;
It is the breath by which the future looks,
The seed of thought where human spirit slept.

It builds a bridge from ignorance to light,
A compass guiding ships through time and space;
It arms the soul with courage for the fight,
And plants compassion deep in every place.

The scholar's quest is not to hoard or bind,
But set the captive wings of wisdom free;
To shape the heart, to elevate the mind,
And serve the truth with fearless dignity.

O learning, sovereign gift to humankind,
You are the crown by which we all are defined.

Sky's Diary

Endless sky, free birds in the fading afternoon,
The sun departs into its crimson circle.
Sitting on the lawn, watching pure wonders,
Old and young alike become enchanted.

The moon smiles - on a full-moon night,
O friend of the night, you glide through silence.
On the sky's canvas, countless stars,
Filling the ledger of time with deeds and dreams.

At dawn, I wake to the call of the magpie robin,
Sparrows and starlings linger by the window path.
With love and longing, I sit in the veranda,
The sound of spoon and cup reminds me
I dwell in this world.

Through the twilight, memories return like echoes,
Faces of yesterday bloom in the quiet air.
The sky becomes a diary of vanished hours,
Yet each star holds a story that still lives here.

At the Edge of the Sea

At the foot of dreams drifts a harbor veiled in haze,
Where longing anchors but never lands.
Through the quiet corridors of pine,
I walk as if through time itself -
Slow, deliberate, unafraid of silence.

On hope's bright shore I rest,
My fingers sifting the patient sands,
Counting the breaths of the sea -
Perhaps to find a pearl,
Perhaps the glint of a hidden gold.

In the far deeps, a ship lifts its masts toward the sky,
Its silhouette a hand that waves me closer,
Yet it stands apart,
Its gaze fixed on the land as though on a promise
It dares not break.

It carries a hundred hopes, sealed away,
Too fragile to touch the body's realm -
Seen only as a shadow across the horizon.
Light boats drift in rhythm with the pulse of the tide,
The sun sinks slowly,
Its red farewell spilling across the water's cheek.

The wind, like a secret messenger,
Glides along the skin of the sea,
Whispering shan-shan to the listening shore.
The waves crash like the clash of distant armies,
Breaking upon the sands where wounds do not heal.

Here, in the harbor of triumph, sorrow drops its anchor.
And in a still pool, where no storm should dwell,
Fate lets surface - without warning -
A great, shadowed shark.

Court of Mercy

The book of life is scarred with stains of sin,
And by inscribing them in its pages-
I became a defendant in the Court of the Creator.
I do not know how to be freed,
Yet I believe my Prophet (ﷺ) will protect me.

On the dreadful Day of the Hereafter-
He is my refuge,
He is the pillar of hope amidst the storm of Judgment.
Still, beneath the burden of deeds,
I search for the gates of mercy.

Ink of repentance spills upon every page,
Yet whispers of hope resound in the soul:
The Lord of Mercy abandons no one,
The Lord of Light turns no one away.

On that day, when every secret will be unveiled,
And every heart will tremble in silence,
I pray my record grows light with forgiveness,
That my sins may be veiled by His compassion.

For in His mercy lies the only shelter,
And in His love - the eternal peace.

When the scales stand before my eyes,
And angels bear witness to truth,
I will yearn for a single drop from His ocean of grace,
To wash away the dust of countless faults.

Through the intercession of the Beloved (ﷺ),
I hope to cross the bridge with ease -
For no soul survives by deeds alone,
Only by the mercy of Ar-Rahman is salvation found.

Avelina

Avelina - your absence is a sorrow
That lingers like twilight in the heart.
To gaze, unblinking, where you once stood
Is a grief the soul can scarcely bear.

In the Coral Jasmine groves, on mornings kissed with dew,
In mango orchards washed in full-moon light,
I see you still -
Your laughter spilling, bright and unrestrained,
Like a river freed from its banks.

When winter's migrant birds return,
Your presence drifts among their wings,
Your shadow glides between their songs.

Roses speak your name in whispers,
The ancient ironwood - eighty winters old -
Only gazes and smiles in knowing silence.

I am as I was -
Untouched by change,
Still standing in the shape your memory left.

Time has shifted,
The world has turned -
Yet, Avelina,
Your light remains unchanged.

At Life's Sunset

The hour tolls -
a life of ceaseless labor draws its final breath.
All possessions scatter,
swept by the restless winds of change.
In the dim hush of dying,
fear sits close, whispering.

By the bedside,
loved ones keep vigil through a sleepless night.
A drowsy dawn
presses fire into weary eyes -
and after a thousand years of living,
it is but one fleeting night.

Elixirs sipped,
the finest grapes,
and even nature herbs -
all fail at sunset,
every remedy slipping away.
Now, with body, mind, and voice,
the younger kneels before the Almighty.

Life's long ledger lies open -
bargains over gains and losses,
a hundred stories,
a hundred wounds.
The heart trembles,
yearning for a single answering gaze,
while the ink of memory
turns pale.

The dry, frail,
withered frame lies still,
shivering on its snow-white bed.
The soul -
a bird unbound -
takes wing
and turns to stone.

Scarlet

Flame of the forest - you are so fair,
So lovely is *butea monosperma's* gaze;
In your love are spellbound - young and old,
Women and men, and even the wistful child,
Though famine may gnaw at the land.

From afar they marvel at your graceful stance,
Yet, nearing you, they all withdraw;
A blossom you are - adorning the garden's heart,
Your clustered petals shining in radiant glory.

Ah, you will not know - but I have known the human soul:
They seek only fragrance, honour,
In all things, as in their food and drink.

Perhaps you think, perhaps you blame Nature -
Yet Nature has bestowed upon so many
A flawless form, a pure and perfect frame;
And still, somehow, fulfilment never came.

Debonair

A handsome young man, phone in hand,
Jeans on his legs, a T-shirt on his back,
Latest bike, speed unstoppable.

A restless heart, trembling eyes,
Woodland shoes, Ray-Ban specs,
Clean-shaven face, a necklace on his neck,
Broad shoulders, wide chest,
An eager gaze, a glossy chin.

The sharp scent of Parisian perfume,
A soul devoted to serving society,
Colorful dreams, sky-high wishes,
Restlessly searching for doe-eyed beauty.

Busy day and night, busy at dawn,
No time for household chores,
But tireless for others' sake,
Surrounded by friends,
Standing there, eyes wandering
Under the excuse of work.

Fast food, cold drinks,
Words flowing like a Romeo's,
From the depths below to the skies above,
Crowds, circles of friends -
Yet in the end, loneliness.

Love-sick in longing, frozen in sorrow,
The pace of life slowed,
A heartbeat without rhythm.

Urban Garden

Paved paths and benches neat,
At the heart, a grand, still pool,
Shade trees small yet sweetly placed,
Lawns trimmed like a gentle dream -
A haven to walk, to rest,
To sip the breeze at leisure.

Youth in chatter, laughter, play,
Late afternoon a little fair,
Elders weaving endless tales,
Young men humming low with talk,
Old friends gathered,
Mothers-in-law unspooling seven sagas,
Wives in whispers, children crawling,
Tea cups clinking now and then,
Or the hum of some small meeting.

The water lies - deep, dark, serene,
Eyes drift toward it, thought-bound, still.
The air is calm, tender, tinged with drowse,
And as the last light thins away,
The garden yields to the lilting chorus of birds.

Memories in the Flow

Thames, Tyne or Tiber, Mississippi or Mackenzie,
Ganges, Godavari or Yamuna, Brahmaputra or Barak -
Endless waters whisper past,
Rivers keep singing; they rush and they roll,
While I remain, only watching.
While I sit watching, in the silence of my soul.

Cruel fate steals so many away;
To hold them in memory is a burden of the heart.
Begum Rokeya, Sofia Kamal,
Nazrul, Michael, and rebels untamed -
So many words, so many dreams linger,
So many voices still call through the air.

They still echo within;
Will there come a day
Will there be a time to meet them out there?
Dreams drift onward, yet deep down I know.
We're all just part of the rivers that flow.
When we meet them once more.

Celestial Wonders

The clouds drift gently, cradling her to their breast.
Shy as a veiled bride, she withdraws,
Slipping into her secret chamber
At the sun's triumphant arrival -
Thus flows the eternal household of the heavens.

Venus glides across the blazing sun -
A rare and wondrous jewel of the cosmos.
The moon steps between the earth and sun -
Ah, the hush of a solar eclipse!
These are the marvels of a vast celestial home,
Where bliss and sorrow, clash and embrace,
Whispers and storms weave their tale.

Orbits traced, revolutions spun,
Positions shifting, places exchanged -
All obey the fixed decree of time,
A measured dance, unbroken, profound,
The household of the sky in eternal motion.

Iron-wood

Before our home it stands beside the lane,
A guardian tree with blossoms pure and white,
Through sunlit days and seasons filled with rain,
Its shade became our shelter and delight.

Beneath its boughs we wandered, young and free,
Our footsteps echoed softly on the ground;
The fragrant Iron wood, a memory,
That bound our souls where simple joys were found.

The road was narrow, yet it seemed so wide,
For every path was graced by branches high;
Its petals fell like stars at eventide,
A quiet blessing drifting from the sky.

O Ironwood of Ceylon, strong and true,
Our lives are marked by all we shared with you.

Princess

I gaze with wistful eyes
Into the void; the vast emptiness; the blue of the sky.

Surely you're seated on the southern balcony,
Far from me - in the realm of my reverie.

I have returned to the pavilion,
To the open courtyard painted in dream's dominion.
Do not think of me,
Do not hold me in your heart secretly.

Now I am alone, deeply alone,
All the rivers of the world flow on, winding, unknown.

You've gone away - far, far away - joined with
The rhythm, melody, and harmony of life's myth.

I am calm, I am serene, I am full of hope,
May remain just there - ever the Princess in your royal scope.

Envy

Envy is a fire unseen,
Burning the heart, unsettling the sheen.
Another's triumph, a thorn to the eye,
It drowns the soul in shadows nearby.

Their laughter strikes the ear with pain,
Their joy awakens wounds again.
Envy's a shadow, bitter and wild,
It fades the colors where love once smiled.

But envy, when shaped with noble desire,
Can lift the soul and set it afire.
If others' brilliance sparks inspiration,
It turns life's grief into aspiration.

Envy - a sword with edges two,
One brings the night, the other, the dew.
The one who transforms it with love's own art,
Is the one who conquers the human heart.

Envy's a flame in shadow's disguise,
It burns in the glow of others' rise.
Yet the one who molds it through patient strife,
Finds in its ashes the truest life.

The Nebula

The rainbow is tinted in seven hues.
You are the nebula, a flame in human souls -
A beacon of light on the edge of darkness.

Countless stars adorn the sky's dome,
Beneath this open firmament, so many are homeless.
You bring joy to the sorrowful -
Like a full moon gazing upon the azure heavens.

The sea beckons me with a gesture,
Its waves soothe away all pain.
The shore is but a bed of sand,
Yet your presence makes it so enchanting.

At the green foothills of the mountain
Where the sky seems to end,
Like the Persian carpet unrolled -
By your presence, I feel truly blessed.

Expectation

A car, a house, a staircase to the sky,
Dreams built of promise, reaching high.
A little hope, a lovely home,
Yet after struggles - despair finds room.

Everyday life teeters on the edge,
Though seemingly stable, it clings to a ledge.
So clever, yet chaos quietly reigns,
No kingdom is his, though the crown he claims.

A beautiful nest, a place called home,
But deep inside, the heart feels alone.
Walls may glitter, the roof may shine,
Yet emptiness lingers between each line.

Dreams once golden now gather dust,
Promises fade into broken trust.
Laughter echoes, but never stays,
Shadows grow longer with passing days.

In chasing the world, the soul lost its way,
Yearning for dawn, yet trapped in gray.
But a flicker of faith still warms the night,
A whisper within that calls to the light.

For beyond despair, new dreams can grow,
Like rivers returning, like seeds that know.
Expectation falters, but hope takes flight,
And through the darkness - emerges the light.

Eileen

I love the one who loves me,
I stay close to the one who longs to keep me near.
I search for her across this wide world -
In cities and villages, across deserts and distant frontiers.

I've tried a little, but haven't searched to my limits,
Maybe I will find her, maybe I won't - haven't thought too deeply.
Haven't found one who matches my mind, nor seen anyone just right.

Perhaps I'll find her nearby, or far away,
Perhaps she's lost in a crowd - alone amidst many.

Once a palmist read my hand with great flair,
Said, "You'll marry late, so be aware."

The one meant for me - perhaps she's not ready yet,
Not yet prepared to join the struggles of life just yet.

Desire

Man dreams in sleep and in imagination,
Hopes to rise, in glory and self-affirmation.
Reality, however, is harsh and steep,
Each step forward hides troubles deep.

Yet still he strives with earnest endeavor,
Thirsting to reach the goal, ceasing never.
In this modern age, it's all competition -
Few extend a hand, or show compassion.

But within the heart a flame keeps burning,
A steadfast light for the soul's yearning.
Though storms may rage and shadows fall,
Desire lifts the spirit above them all.

Dreams may falter, paths may bend,
Yet hope abides till journey's end.
For every wound, for every scar,
Tells how strong our desires are.

Tale of the Seasons

Autumn is truly a delight -
Yet spring, even more so!
Spring is the fluttering spirit
Of a youthful heart in full glow.

Winter comes veiled in mist,
Like an aged man fading slow -
Wrapped from head to toe,
Resisting the morning chill
That reddens a boy's cheek aglow.

But with winter's fading breath,
Spring arrives with birdsong bright -
Among the trees, a joyful choir,
And by the lake, beneath the palms,
Lovers whisper, friends unite,
Readying for a forest picnic, hearts alight.

And summer, radiant sovereign of flame,
Pours golden fire across the land;
Fields of wheat sway in reverent bow,
Oceans shimmer at her command.
Children chase the dragonfly's flight,
Travelers seek horizons new -
Beneath her sun, the world expands,
Dreams awaken, bold and true.

The Boatman

I am the ferryman,
Carrying souls across - I must agree to serve.
I eat a little, sleep a while,
And when someone comes, I set the boat adrift.

This side is riverbank, the other a crumbling land,
By the river's curve, a kingfisher takes a stand.

So many things float by,
I watch them, and thus life goes by.

Mornings are tender, serene in hue,
Noon burns with a fierce bright view,
Evening is charming, full of grace,
Night - mysterious, in a dreamlike space.

In autumn, the river is calm and still,
Its waters gentle, with a quiet will.

In monsoon, the river breaks all bounds,
A torrential force with roaring sounds.

In winter, fog hides the river's face,
The sun appears in a ghostly trace.

The river of death - **Vessel** - vast and wide,
Its body harsh; worn down with pride.
No friend, no gondolier on its side.

Dedicated to the language martyrs of 1368
Bengal's 5th Jaishthya, May 19th of 1961

My Essence

I stand by Bengal, and sing in Bangla.
I weep in Bangla, and my soul thrives in Bangla.

Bangla is my entire being.
Bangla is my inner soul.
I dream in Bangla.
I write stories in Bangla.

I take pride in Bangla - it is my meditation.
My body, mind, and soul find peace in Bangla songs.

I know how to laugh in Bangla.
I wish to die in Bangla.

Bangla is my mother's tongue.
Bangla is my daughter's tongue.

The fish curry of Bengal.
The water lily in the lake.

The beauty of the Bengali women's attire.
A champa flower tucked in her hair bun.

Water lilies in the lake.
Mango buds in the mango orchard.

Jari, Shari, and Baul folk songs.
The glory of Siraj and Lalon lives on.

Bengal's embroidered Nakshi Kantha (quilt).
Tales of immortal brave warriors.

Bangla is rich with poetic essence.
The river islands (chars) of Bengal are fertile with silt.

Bengal's Poush festival, Bengal's Nabanna - with
siddha puli, pathi sapta, and ending with sweet desserts.

Apathy

I look at the sky -
that endless blue sky -
and gaze as far as my eyes allow.
I look with tired, bored eyes,
wondering how many words,
how many sorrows,
how many lives are tangled there.

How many words,
how many aches,
how many memories,
how much forgetfulness.

The colorful moments of life,
the golden days gone by -
they drift like shadows in my mind.
My heart mourns in silence,
but I cannot speak
neither in solitude,
nor in these loud faubourgs.

Welkin

You are the sky, you are the abyss,
I am restless, I am adrift in bliss.
You are the beginning, you are the end,
I am distracted, confused without a friend.

You are colorful, I am pale,
You are lively, I am frail.
You are a dream, you are gold,
I am weary, my spirit old.

You are beauty, you are clear,
I am vile, to be feared.
You are gentle, you are wise,
I am ashamed, with sorrow in my eyes.

You are the morning's radiant flame,
I am the shadow without a name.
You are the river, ceaseless, free,
I am the stone, drowning in the sea.

You are the song the night-bird sings,
I am the silence of broken wings.
You are the hope the future bears,
I am the burden of endless cares.

You are eternal, vast, divine,
I am a moment, lost in time.
Yet in my darkness, one truth I see:
Without your light - what is left of me?

Testimony

The book of life is marked by the stain of sin.
By putting sins in the account of life -
I became a defendant in the court of *The Creator*.
I don't know how to get over it,
I have faith that my Prophet (pbuh) will save me,
In time of crisis in the Hereafter -
HE is the one who trusts,
HE is the trust in the day of severe judgement.

Yet, beneath the weight of my own deeds,
I search for a door of mercy.
The ink of regret bleeds on every page,
But hope keeps whispering in my soul:
The Lord of Mercy never abandons,
The Lord of Light never refuses.

On that Day, when every secret is unveiled,
And every heart trembles in its silence,
I pray my account is softened by forgiveness,
That my sins are veiled by His Compassion.
For in His Mercy lies the only refuge,
And in His Love - the eternal peace

Life Still Endures

Still the North Star rises in the sky,
The moon smiles, dawn breaks, birds sing.
Still the clouds gather, the rain falls,
And the earth, bathed in rain, grows fertile.
Still children laugh, and flowers bloom.

For flowers bloom, and fruits are born,
Still rivers flow, floods rise, silt settles.
Islands fill, valleys bear harvests,
Still mankind finds joy in sky-born dreams,
And wanders in imagined worlds with delight.

Still tears flow and wet the heart,
Yet love touches souls and keeps them alive.
Still the music plays, the flute hums,
And life seeks dawn in melodies of hope.

Still the scent of paddy drifts in the breeze,
The farmer's sweat ripens the dream of harvest.
Still the lamps burn in nights of darkness,
Guiding mankind with hope toward the morning.

The Battlefield of Taste

Old greens, old garb -
Even fish kaliya feels passé.
Stews, six-spice fritters, luchis, chili's tease -
We crave instead: chili chicken, idli, dosa,
And a steaming biryani feast.

Old-school dishes don't tempt us now,
Without "food" and "dish," hearts won't allow.
Burgers, sandwiches, soda in hand -
A carnival feel, though born of Indian land.

The palate has forsaken flavor for "taste,"
What once was rich now feels misplaced.
Homegrown dishes seem to fade,
Foreign cravings now invade -
A Western tide sweeps our plate.

Hot sauce, chili sauce - European flair,
Even stir-fried veggies echo foreign air.
Slowly we're shifting, eastward perhaps,
Yet native essence eludes our grasp.

Khorma-pulao, Kashmiri delight,
Gujarati, Goan, Mughlai might.
Pickles, chutneys, koftas, kebabs -
A sacred burst on the tongue, divine as gods,
With spices sharp like heavenly swords.

Hilsa with potatoes? Heresy, they say!
Ginger with raw banana - culinary dismay.
Yet hilsa roe with green papaya - what grace!
Magur fish and banana - an unmatched taste.

Nectar-like dishes stir the soul,
Even as bile shivers in salted bowl.
In subtle spice and measured flame,
Winter's pabda curry earns its fame -
Finished with coriander's green acclaim.

Tender neem leaves, bitter and pure,
Astringent joys that quietly endure.
Like poetry's nine moods - navarasa lore -
Food, too, has six tastes in Ayurveda's core.

My Vision

I have seen the sky so close,
And the rainbow painted in colors of imagination,
The ocean in its own rhythm and pose.

I have seen the Great One in His own glory!
A child in innocence, pure in story,
The orbit in its unique harmony,
And the railway in its parallel symmetry.

I have seen the trees in service of man,
The showers nurturing harvest and grain,
The sun and the moon in the limits of rule,
But man - I have not seen in his own true soul.

I have seen the wind in its endless stream,
The river flowing in its destined scheme,
Yet man I have not seen in his truest light -
Shrouded in pride, lost from sight.

Embroidered Quilt

So many words about life -
Yet death carries a hundred pains.

Life - it's a patchwork quilt of hope,
Life - it's the terror of simply being alive.

I've seen much of what's to be seen,
And missed what remains unseen.
The memories of the past are sweet,
The imagined future - richly replete.

So many have told me tales,
So many have shown me dreams.
The dear ones only made me ponder -
They've seized well upon my moments of weakness.

A deep sigh - that is my final solace.
I'm well, I'm happy -
With you, and in your likeness, I remain.

Kids

Lovely kid jumping on the grassland,
Rising calf doing the same.
Little puppy barking on the street,
Kitten hiding beneath the bin.

Ducklings swimming across the pool,
While chickens wander on the bank.
Goslings marching beside the lake,
Fawn darting lightly through the glade.

Colt searching for water in the desert,
Calf splashing freely in a tiny stream.
Lambs skipping over the meadow,
Piglets rolling in the mud with glee.

Whelp gazing eager at the den,
Cub peeking with a smiling face.
Foals chasing shadows in the sunshine,
Chicks chirping softly near their nest.

River

Oh River, thou giver of fertile vales,
Thou who dost bless the lands with fruitful trails;
Oh River, O River, thou mighty stream,
Sustainest life and nurtures every dream.

Oh River, cut not the lives of humble men,
Uproot not their dwellings, nor their glen;
Thou art the lifeblood of the artisan's hand,
Granting joy and solace across the land.

Oh River, thy waters, both fierce and kind,
Bear hope to the weary, ease to the mind;
Forever flow, O River, thy sacred way,
Bestow thy blessings, day by endless day.

Oh River, in thy bosom secrets lie,
Reflecting the moon, the stars in the sky;
Thou whisperest tales of ages gone,
And cradleth the dawn with thy gentle song.

Oh River, thou art the mirror of time,
Thy murmuring waves, a soft, eternal rhyme;
Guide the wanderer, comfort the lost,
And teach mankind the value of thy cost.

Bloom

Creation of varieties! O season,
If a bud comes, can a flower be far behind?
I love winter and spring -
More than all,
At dawn, it rests upon the desk;
Oh, blind, you'll see in the dark.

I love the brave and young,
All the straightforward lungs.
If a bud comes, can a flower be far behind?

Soft rains whisper secrets to the soil,
And the wind hums tunes of tomorrow.
Each petal unfolds like a quiet promise,
Each leaf stretches toward the sun.

The river hums a gentle hymn,
Carrying dreams downstream.
Even in frost, life waits patiently,
Knowing warmth will arrive.

I watch the sparrow learn to fly,
The child chasing shadows in the afternoon.
Every heartbeat is a small revolution,
Every breath, a step toward light.

If a bud comes, can a flower be far behind?
Hope rises where courage dwells,
And even in darkness, the soul blooms,
Soft, brave, eternal, ever young.

Patriarch

A father is the steadfast tree,
Rooted firm in constancy.
Through storms of life, through sun and rain,
He bears the weight, endures the strain.

Silent architect of unseen dreams,
He builds with patience, brick by beams.
Not through words, but deeds convey
The love that guides us, day by day.

His hands, though worn, uphold our sky,
His faith restores when hopes run dry.
In trials fierce, his shoulders stand,
A fortress strong, a steady hand.

No throne he seeks, no crown of gold,
Yet in his strength, our world unfolds.
The lamp he lights, though small in flame,
Burns on through years, a noble name.

He is the path where courage flows,
The soil where seeds of virtue grow.
Within his care, the future thrives,
A legacy of steadfast lives.

A father - the quiet, guarding flame,
An unsung hero, honored name.
Though time may pass, one truth remains:
His timeless bond flows through our veins.

Eternal Motherly Love

Mother - an eternal stream of nectar,
The first touch of life, tender and pure.
Her voice, a lullaby; her embrace, a sleep,
In her warm heart, all worries fall deep.

She is the dawn, awakening each day,
She is the sky, vast in her sway.
She is the sun, shedding light endless,
She is the moon, soothing and selfless.

In her silent sacrifice blooms the future,
In her love lies the essence of human nature.
Not a royal throne, nor treasures untold,
Her affection alone is a crown of gold.

Her weary hands carry blessings unseen,
Her whispered prayers keep the world serene.
Through every struggle, her spirit shines bright,
Guiding the lost with a mother's light.

She is the tree whose roots run deep,
Her shade a shelter where tired souls sleep.
Her tears unseen water the earth,
Her smile alone gives dreams their birth.

Mother - an ocean of endless love,
Where countless drops of sweetness move.
Her eyes shine like eternal stars,
Sacred, gentle, no shadow mars.

Mother - the song the soul remembers,
A flame that glows through fading embers.
In every breath, in every prayer,
The eternal Mother's love is there.

A Fleeting Hope

Yet Barun has accepted it all -
His parents are gone,
He lives with someone,
Works in a factory,
His sister was in college.

His childhood was painted in many hues,
But the present is utterly somber.
Five years have passed -
His sister became an engineer.

Then suddenly, fate struck -
A road accident took her away.
All pride, all hope of life
Was swallowed by darkness and despair.

Yet Barun lives on,
Clinging to the memory of his sister close to his heart.

Ephemeral Fire

Youth is a kind of madness,
And some, it seems, are minions of the devil -
It's a drunkenness without wine,
Like bats in the night.

Through colorful eyes, the youth sees a dazzling world.
They speak in the rhythm of poetry,
They hum through the lyrics of songs.
Time turns them into poets,
Moved by emotion, they become one.

With generous hearts, they help others,
Through storms, rain, and endless clouds.

The dreamy days of life,
The moments of bliss we left behind -
Once gone, they never return.
We won't just sit and wait for brighter days.

Youth is painted in a thousand hues,
Yet even more vibrant is childhood in comparison.

The Last Meeting

You are standing beside me,
While I sit near you -
You're gazing intently at me,
At the arches of my silent eyes.

I wonder why you watch me so,
As if I cannot hold you in my world anymore.
Even if for a moment we belong to each other,
After that fleeting instant - two shores, two souls.

The platform stretches long and endless,
To the east - where the guest house stands -
The scent of flowers drifts gently in the air.

Locking eyes with mine -
What use is there, just to see?
Beloved, this is the last time we'll meet,
So everything around feels empty, incomplete.

Toward the Pained Gaze

You -
Why do you gaze that way,
Into my sorrow-laden eyes?
Tears drift like clouds across the sky,
A flame consumes the forest of my mind,
And I remain - forgetting the soul within.

You -
Why do you gaze that way,
Into my sorrow-laden eyes?
Crickets sing in the shiuli grove,
A shepherd rests beneath the shade,
Honor, name, and kin are lost -
Nothing remains, all has slipped away.

You -
Why do you gaze that way,
Into my sorrow-laden eyes?
Flowers smile at the crimson dawn,
Birdsong stirs the waking world,
Yet my heart lies still in slumber -
Why, I know not; drowsiness lingers on.

You -
Why do you gaze that way,
Into my sorrow-laden eyes?

The Late Blooming Love

I love the one who loves me,
I stay close to the one who longs to keep me near.
I search for her across this wide world -
In cities and villages, across deserts and distant frontiers.

I've tried a little, but haven't searched to my limits;
Maybe I will find her, maybe I won't -
Haven't thought too deeply.
Haven't found one who matches my mind,
Nor seen anyone just right.

Perhaps I'll find her nearby, or far away,
Perhaps she's lost in a crowd -
Alone amidst many.

Once a palmist read my hand with great flair,
Said, *"You'll marry late, so be aware."*
The one meant for me - perhaps she's not ready yet,
Not yet prepared to join the struggles of life.

Inner Fire

Why do flowers
turn their faces toward you,
as if no other sun exists?
Why do the stars
prick the fabric of night,
just to glimmer in your name?

Why does the first crimson light
smile through the bilva leaves,
and why does the bird's chest
flutter with midday joy,
spilling its song into the air?

Why does the shepherd boy
lift his flute when you pass?
Why does the moon itself
curve into laughter at your sight?

What storm of feeling,
what unseen tide,
shakes the soul from its nest?
How does the lotus root
find ground in the lake's abyss?

Why does the ocean
heave with sudden tide
the instant it beholds you?
Why does the hidden fire within
fall silent, like a flame blown out?

In the fevered chords
of a global song,
you strike rhythm in restless minds;
and even the hands of laborers pause -
as towns awaken at your presence.

You stir a rhythm in the restless mind;
work halts in the hands of laborers
when you are seen within the town.

Elegy for the Present

The times have shifted -
Seasons have lost their soul.
No rains arrive with monsoon,
No winter breath turns cold.

Vegetables taste of nothing,
The rainbow fades, grown pale.
Life has lost its essence,
The pulse within grows frail.

Children no longer weep,
And laughter no longer heals.
Learning sinks in measure,
While wealth ascends in worth.

Trust is broken,
And promises fall to earth.
Trees bear no harvest,
Many fruits are unseen.

Illness knows no ending,
Yet the wicked never leave.
The jobless crowd is swelling,
Even computer hands are cut.

The world shrinks to a palm -
Through email and internet.
The noble fade away,
Yet leave their lasting mark.

Railway lines are stolen
By the lawless, by the stark.
Man turns against his brother,
Life is played like a game.

Shops rise without license,
Bank accounts still gain.
The hungry die in silence,
While a few grow fat with gold.

Yet mankind endures -
Though shadows weigh us down,
We wait with fragile hope
That good days may unfold.

Woven Fabric

You are the sky, you are the abyss,
I am restless, I am adrift in bliss.
You are the beginning, you are the end,
I am distracted, confused without a friend.

You are colorful, I am pale,
You are lively, I am frail.

You are a dream, you are gold,
I am weary, my spirit old.

You are beauty, you are clear,
I am vile, to be feared.

You are gentle, you are wise,
I am ashamed, with sorrow in my eyes.

I had loved you with great devotion,
And you, too, had loved me - if only a little.

I had hoped to bury my face in your veil,
To weave a nest of happiness in every fold of life's tide.

You didn't know - you were already a young woman,
No longer, in others' eyes, the little girl you once were.

Then one day, all of a sudden,
In the courtyard I saw a bright red woven fabric
And a finely adorned carriage.

That you knew how to wear a woven fabric-
Even I had never known that.

Nature's Symphony

The mountain brook begins to sing,
With silver light its waters bring.
The golden sun, through branches high,
Spreads its smile across the sky.

The pine and cedar, tall and still,
Guard the road by the mountain hill.
The gentle wind, so fresh, so clear,
Breathes its calm to all who hear.

The river hums in crystal tone,
Through pebbled beds its song is sown.
A sacred hymn, so pure, so deep,
In nature's heart its echoes sleep.

At dawn the birds awake the land,
Their chorus vast, their notes so grand.
And in this symphony divine,
The soul and nature intertwine.

The Desolate Highway

The sound of rain reminds me of you,
The whooshing wind - reminds me of you.
Soft, serene footsteps remind me of you,
Standing still - kamini and kanchan flowers -
remind me of you.

The clouds remind me of you,
The waves, too, remind me of you.
The jingling of anklets calls back your memory,
The chirping of birds sings your name to me.

Why is this highway so deserted today?
Why is this vibrant town so lifeless now?
Why is this cultural arena so void of voices?
Why is this institute of learning so abandoned?

Do you still enjoy parting your braid in two?
Do you still tie that loose, carefree bun?
Does that curved gaze still linger between your brows?
Does your walk still sway with the wind, like before?

Your lips - like a flowing boat,
Your cheeks - two blooming gardens,
Your face - like the sunrise over Simla,
And your eager, frenzied gaze - like a restless Chatak
bird longing for the rain.

These days, when you open the window - what do you see?
Do you flip through the pages of your favorite novel - what do you find?
What do you see inside those delicate Chinese cups and plates at the dining table?
What reflection meets your eyes in the life-sized bathroom mirror?

Life becomes a broken fraction in arithmetic - when you are not there.
Civilization and history crumble - when you are not there.
Youth fades into ascetic withdrawal - when you are not there.
The harbor of the heart is engulfed in smoke - when you are not there.

The rain is just the same, the darkness still remains.
The Barak still flows beneath the hills.
The early morning MTC bus to Shillong still departs.
The chill of the dawn wind is just the same.

There was once a flute in my heart -
it hasn't played for years.
There was once a mirror in my heart - I haven't seen myself in it for so long.

Now, when I open the window, I see a sea before me -
A sea of emptiness, a sea of ruin.
From the ocean of your memory, a silent glance drifts to my doorstep -
And my little boat floats in that gaze.

Lantern of the Heart

May you never grow indifferent or silent,
your voice always stirring,
a breeze that moves through still hearts,
never fading into shadow,
O radiant soul.

May you never become lifeless or dull,
like the ocean stripped of color,
or the horizon drained of light;
let your spirit ripple with quiet brilliance,
O shining flame.

May thoughtless apathy never touch you,
may carelessness and aimless wandering
never cloud your mind;
let wisdom and tender thought
dance in your gaze,
O gentle light.

May the powerless, the spiritless, the untalented
never crowd around your path;
let only those who honor beauty, courage, and heart
walk near your light,
O kindred spirit.

May restless, immobile, detached indifference
never brush past you;
may every moment embrace you with life,
and even in silence,
may your presence shimmer like a lantern
guiding hearts that seek warmth,
O eternal flame.

Where my Root Lie

By the silvered banks of the Kushiyara flows my town,
Where the Raj Bungalow rests, the Dak Bungalow stands,
And the Martyr's Arch rises in solemn grace -
Once a proud sub-division of Sylhet,
Famed far beyond its borders.

Shombhu, Kailash, Romoni, Asad -
Like waters from four oceans, yet tasting the same,
Mingling in calm, in peace, in joy;
A tranquil land beneath a tender sky,
Its edges dressed in quiet beauty.

Here, Muslim, Hindu, Christian -
Weave their lives in the same unbroken thread
Of harmony, unity, and compassion.
Mosque, temple, and church stand shoulder to shoulder,
And no wall rises between the rich and the poor.

Sky's Diary

Endless sky, free birds in the fading afternoon,
The sun departs into its crimson circle.
Sitting on the lawn, watching pure wonders,
Old and young alike become enchanted.

The moon smiles - on a full-moon night,
O friend of the night, you glide through silence.
On the sky's canvas, countless stars,
Filling the ledger of time with deeds and dreams.

At dawn, I wake to the call of the magpie robin,
Sparrows and starlings linger by the window path.
With love and longing, I sit on the porch,
The sound of spoon and cup reminds me I dwell in this world.

And in the hush of twilight's return,
when earth softens under a veil of blue,
the sky whispers back my forgotten prayers,
teaching me that each day is both an ending
and a gentle beginning anew.

Muskaan – ***a Bengali New Year's Gift***

On the morning the New Year first awoke,
Heaven smiled, and a blessing spoke.
Little Muskaan came into this light,
A blossom born on Boishakh's bright.

Her skin, like silk, so tender and fair,
Cheeks like petals beyond compare.
Blue-tinted eyes with a gentle gleam,
Her smile - sweet Sameehah's dream.

The rain that fell on Boishakh's night,
Still lingers within my heart so bright.
For when Muslihah graced the earth that day,
I stood for children's joy in play.

O precious niece, joy of our line,
Your laughter rings, a gift divine.
In every glance, in every tone,
You make our hearts your cherished home.

May New Year's dawn forever recall,
The day you came - the best gift of all.
A star of hope, a tender flame,
Muskaan, forever bless your name.

India : A Patriotic Poem

India - my pride, my eternal flame,
In your soil lives history's name.
From Himalayan peaks to the ocean's span,
You embody the spirit, the soul of man.

Your rivers, your forests, your boundless skies,
Awaken strength where true hope lies.
Through fires of struggle, through sacrifice vast,
You taught the nation a will to last.

Freedom is etched in martyrs' breath,
Glory shines brighter than fear of death.
You are not merely a land to adore -
You are our spirit, forevermore.

In your voice resounds the call of one,
Beyond all faith, beneath the sun.
Unity in diversity, timeless and grand,
India, the torch of peace across the land.

The Threshold

The doorbell of my heart rings-
loud, insistent, unrelenting.
Tell me-
which door should I open first?

Suddenly, the outer bell rings.
On one side of the door-*you.*
On the other side-*me.*

In a moment, I will open it.
You may turn out to be my beloved,
Or a long-lost relative,
Or even an enemy.

When the threshold opens-
A new acquaintance may begin,
Your sight may scorch my eyes with contempt,
Or bring tears of joy rushing down.

Or-
Your hands may cause me harm.

Two doors wait before me:
The world's, and the heart's.
Which one
Should I open first?

When Love Turned to Farewell

I had loved you with great devotion,
And you, too, had loved me - if only a little.
I had hoped to bury my face in your veil,
To weave a nest of happiness
in every fold of life's tide.

You didn't know - you were already a young woman,
No longer, in others' eyes,
the little girl you once were.
Your laughter had changed,
your glance carried secrets,
and still I dreamed you belonged only to me.

Then one day, all of a sudden,
In the courtyard I saw a bright red sari
And a finely adorned carriage.
That you knew how to wear a sari -
Even I had never known that.

My heart stood silent,
bewildered between joy and loss.
Was it a dream, or truth unveiled?
The child I loved had drifted away,
and in her place stood
a bride the world was claiming.

And I remained behind,
with my devotion untold,
my hopes scattered like petals in the wind.
Love had not ended,
yet it could no longer stay -
it had turned quietly into farewell.

Daring

A handsome youth, phone in hand,
Jeans worn snug, T-shirt on stand,
Latest bike roaring, wild and free,
Eyes darting, heart in glee.

Woodland shoes, Ray-Ban shades,
Clean-shaven charm, smile pervades,
Broad shoulders, chest so wide,
Gaze intense, chin with pride.

Paris perfume, strong, untamed,
A life devoted, service aimed,
Colorful dreams, sky-flower desire,
Seeking, searching, doe-eyed fire.

Busy days and busy dawns,
No time for home, life's hectic fawns,
For others' sake, he plays his part,
Friendly circles, always at heart.

Fast food bites, cold drinks in hand,
Words flow soft, like Romeo planned,
From underworld depths to skies above,
Societies, friendships, yet lonely love.

In love's longing, in sorrow's chain,
Life's pulse sluggish, dull the strain.

It was 1996, on my second trip to Hawra during a visit to Kolkata, I stayed for a few days. In life's journey we meet so many people - sometimes once, sometimes again and again. And thus -

A Chapter of Memory

I stood at the Sealdah bus stop.
A bus came to rest,
and from its door stepped a middle-aged woman -
a famous novel in one hand,
a pink umbrella in the other,
eyes like sudden petals,
a marigold blooming in her hair.
She looked as though the tides of life
had never broken her shores.

Untroubled by ornaments,
unafraid of shattering pots,
she seemed about to speak -
yet no words came.
Instead, she pressed into my palm
a folded slip of paper - her address.

Clad in spring-yellow,
with restrained speech and an open face,
her heart carried quiet longings.
Beyond the Botanical Garden's gate,
in that old aristocratic house of Shibpur -
I thought to myself,
how perfectly she belonged.

If ever you wander that way,
you may catch sight of me -
by the banks of the Hooghly,
in the quiet edges of B. B. D. Bagh.
Now and then, I pass through;
best not to linger
on life's backward turn.

I think it was long ago -
perhaps at a party,
on an autumn evening -
I first saw you.
A silver glint marked your parting hair,
and then you dissolved
into the crowd of life,
coming to rest only
in the hearth of a beloved home.

Reflection on Contemporary Times

The rhythm of time has altered;
the seasons have been stripped of their essence.
Monsoon no longer brings the rains,
winter has lost its chill.
Vegetables carry no taste,
the rainbow has dimmed its brilliance.

Life itself seems emptied of vitality,
the pulse of being grows faint.
Children no longer cry with innocence,
laughter no longer echoes in human hearts.

Education slides downward,
while the prestige of wealth ascends.
Trust is betrayed,
promises dissolve into falsehood.

Nature too withdraws its gifts -
trees no longer yield fruit,
many once-familiar fruits disappear.
Disease multiplies without end,
yet evil appears immortal.

The jobless multiply in despair,
while even the skilled are dismissed.
The world contracts into a single palm,
through the illusions of email and internet.

The noble and virtuous fade away,
though their immortal legacies remain.
Railway lines fall prey to encroachment,
seized by antisocial forces.

Humanity turns upon itself,
life is reduced to a game of chance.
Unlicensed ventures thrive,
bank balances swell regardless.

The hungry continue to perish,
while the few hoard wealth without remorse.
And yet, mankind endures -
perhaps because hope still whispers
that better days are near.

Red Tape

A sharp word -
sometimes it helps,
unlocking the knot of work,
sweeping away delay,
till the current flows free.

The binding threads of red tape -
the body grows numb to them,
tedious, endless,
requests, reminders, repeated pleas -
yet nothing moves.

At times it seems
the task will never be done,
and still, one must return.

Patience shatters,
its dam breaks wide,
and fear disappears.

Hope - never abandoned,
that sly enchantress -
draws us once more
to look again.

The Window

An artist lingers by the southern frame,
Awakened sudden by fate's soft chime;
Before his eyes, my cherished one appears -
Returned from her father's home to rest awhile.

Dawn

Spring's enchantments scatter the mist of sleep,
Life unfolds its long-forbidden gate;
Morning birdsong weaves the threads of hope,
While memory lays its weight upon the soul.

Noon

Beneath a sun that burns with searing truth,
The weary seeker longs for shade;
Dreams and burdens, twined in sweat and dust,
Yield the harvest every heart has made.

Evening

The sky dissolves in crimson and in ash,
Twilight hums with secrets left untold;
Gain and sorrow mingle in its hymn,
Life inscribes its lessons once again.

Night

The moon reclines upon a silver bed,
Fireflies stitch their light across the dark;
The window is no pane of wood and glass -
It is a passage, where the soul meets itself.

The Crimson Glow

When forehead's crimson hue
glistens in beauty's delight,
you shine so gracefully, adorned with jingling earrings,
like the full moon gleaming in the night sky,
stars shimmering by its side.

Across the face of the earth you stride,
the soil quenches its thirst
by kissing your feet.

In the cosmic array of planets
the radiant dawn spreads its glow,
filling the world with light.

In oceans and seas lie countless pearls and gems,
in lakes and wetlands bloom lilies and birds -
yet seeing you,
hearts are filled with fragrance and charm.

Moonlit nights, dewdrop-laden dawns,
and in the flower groves
resound the golden melody of the cuckoo's call

Veils of Affection

Wrapped in the veil of illusion,
Why have you bound me -
Within your life of joy and prosperity,
In that radiant stream of existence?

Enveloped in tenderness,
Why have you entwined me -
In your tranquil household,
Amid the flowing cascade of family life?

Amid affection,
Why have you given me a place -
In the pure gold of your courtyard,
In that golden bloom of the lotus divine?

With the trust of faith,
Why have you sheltered me -
In your untainted way of being,
Within the blue horizon of your words and deeds?

Eternal Love

Whoever has seen their beloved
In the dim, shadowy glow of light,
In sleep and in dreams,
By day, by night, and in silent thoughts,
In the morning's first light, at dawn's return,
When the sun rises with all, among all, yet
In a secluded intimacy.

Whoever has found their beloved in their own way,
No matter how far apart they may be,
From afar they remember me -
Every moment, every instant,
Consumed by thoughts of me,
Unseen by all, yet dwelling in every heart and home.

Whoever has loved their beloved unreservedly,
And the beloved has loved them back fearlessly,
This love is neither petty nor false,
But pure, extraordinary, and beyond human measure,
Open to all eyes, known to all minds,
Flowing without restraint.

This love is eternal -
Without beginning, without end,
An unceasing devotion in winter, autumn, and spring.
This love is true, noble, and wondrous,
A love that dedicates life itself,
A guiding light for generations to come.

The Pain of Absence

I cannot endure your absence;
I cannot reconcile myself to a life without you.

Though I know perpetual closeness is impossible,
Though I know endless meetings cannot be,
Still my heart wonders:
How will you remain with me?
How shall I keep you before my eyes?

My heart insists on your nearness,
My soul longs for you beside me.

Why this pain, I do not understand;
Why this restless heart, I cannot explain.
Perhaps you can tell me -
Why does my being desire you so endlessly?

I know I possess much in life,
I know that I already have you.
Yet my heart stirs again and again,
And my tears return unbidden.

Do you wish to make me weep?
Do you wish to set me aflame?
Fate once placed a distance between us,
And I too built a wall of silence.
Yet you never allowed me to drift away,
You never let me perish in despair.

Do you not perceive the weight of my sorrow?
Will you not hear the trembling of my words?
For you, beloved, are all-understanding;
You already know the secret language of my soul.

Caitriona

Never be indifferent, never be silent -
this is my wish for you, O Amelia.

Never grow dull like a motionless, waveless sea -
this is my yearning for you, O Olivia.

May apathy, callousness, and thoughtlessness never
touch you -
this is my desire for you, O Sofia.

Let dimness, lifelessness, and lack of talent never draw
near -
this is my longing for you, O Isabella.

May idleness, stillness, and detachment never come
close -
this is my hope for you, O Elena Isabella.

The Stream of Words

So many words I had to tell you,
So many things I longed to share -
But seeing you weep in exhaustion
Left me troubled and lost in care.

All that I wished to narrate to you
Was drowned in your flood of cries,
Leaving me worn and wearied.
Come, sit beside me now,
And listen to the tales of joy and sorrow.

Do not keep gazing far away like that,
For your pained, distant look
Is something my heart cannot bear.
Smile a little, and I will tell you
Of the wondrous and noble creations
The Creator has shaped -
The sky and air, the seas and waters -
Never once straying from His perfect design.

Patricia

I love to walk the river's edge
When the sand is cool and damp beneath my feet.
I love to taste ripe tamarind
When laced with just the right salt and pepper.

I love to hear a song
When the voice and melody flow like silk.
But most of all, I love to join my life with another
When she is Patricia - the one my heart longs for.

A winter night feels like bliss
When the warmth comes from my own cover.
A path strewn with thorns feels soft
When a true companion walks beside me.

The fiercest summer heat feels cool
When the breeze is tender and kind.
Yes - I love to join my life with another
When she is Patricia - the one my heart longs for.

The sky feels within my grasp
When fortune smiles upon me.
The moon feels like my dearest friend
When the dark night glows with light.

A deep lake may look dark
Yet be crystal-clear within.
Oh, I love to join my life with another
When she is Patricia - the one my heart longs for.

I love my own reflection in the mirror
When my form is pleasing to see.
My heart dances
When my body is youthful and strong.

A meal after toil feels like a feast
When digestion is kind and true.
Always, I love to join my life with another
When she is Patricia - the one my heart longs for.

Eyeball

In your eyes, I find my face,
A trembling pulse, a shadowed place.
A burn that stings, a tear that grows,
A hundred thoughts the mind now knows -
Of days to come, of moments near,
Of futures weighed with doubt and fear.
In your voice, my song takes flight,

Its echo warms the edge of night.
A sudden throb through ear and head,
A silver rain on hair is spread-
And in that pain, a joy concealed,
A bliss the heart has never sealed.
Your gentle steps, like snails that glide,
Your shapely arms, your glowing stride.
A beauty born in lifetimes past,
A bond through ages, holding fast-
Yet on the shore of truth's domain,
This silent raft must still remain.

I see a form of whitened grace,
A crescent moon upon your face,
Gold hair that drapes a noble brow,
A memory I can't disavow -
Its threads entwined in mind's deep sea,
Refusing to let go of me.

And still your eyes will stir my core,
Confuse my heart, and pull for more.
A mercy flows, a longing cries -
And still I ask within those eyes:
What power makes me feel this way?
Why must it be, and must it stay?

Futile

Beneath the flyover's shadow, beside the rattling rails,
Mornings wake to the taste of despair,
Evenings sink into the bitter dregs of disillusion-
Life itself a burden, survival a daily war,
In a "developing" land still shackled to its want.

A life without design, a destiny undesired,
Hands outstretched for two scant handfuls of grain;
Days heavy with sorrow, nights thick with dread,
Where weeds twist through rubble,
And broken stones stand like mute sentinels of neglect.

The stench hangs heavy, the air itself hostile,
Every breath a wound to the nostrils;
Behind walls of woven jute,
The sketches of human existence fade and fray,
While plates and bowls, clinking faintly,
Are rinsed in the railway's stagnant, murky ditch.

The Illusion of Time

The bridal night is not mere ritual -
Sweet whispers carry the hours away,
Until dawn presses its fingers
Upon the windowpane.
Joy slips by like flowing water,
But sorrow- sorrow never seems to pass.

A few minutes in the sky,
Stretch into long hours on the road.
Happiness journeys with ease,
Yet on its hills and hollows
We stumble, we fall -
While sorrow never seems to pass.

In the vast universe, Neil Armstrong touched the moon,
But in the universe of marriage
No one is beyond its trials.
The weight of fame makes men weep,
Even golden times may shatter,
Like Indra falling from the heavens -
For sorrow never seems to pass.

Entrance at the Door of Heart

You entered my heart's silent door -
Like a deer wandering into a secret forest,
And this weary soul, wrapped in pain,
Began to dream beneath your gentle steps.

You entered my heart's silent door -
Like a graceful figure by the Dhaleshwari's shore.
Why did you come, veiled in mystery,
Carrying the whisper of death,
Yet awakening the pulse of life within me?

You entered my heart's silent door -
Like a whistling-duck upon Malini's lake,
Gilding the waters with sudden beauty,
Bringing the balm of quiet joy
To a soul long aching in silence.

You entered my heart's silent door -
Like sunlight breaking through sorrow's clouds.
In the breeze of happiness, my spirit sways,
And the chamber of my being
Fills with serene delight.

Endear- Partha

Thou art as sandalwood -
whose fragrance lingers long after the blossom has withered,
whose essence sanctifies the very air it graces.
In the garden of my humble existence,
thou art the solitary rose of deepest crimson,
set apart in beauty and in rarity.

Thine unwavering gaze,
arched beneath the noble sweep of ebon brows;
thy manly hands, clothed with nature's own garment;
thy lips, like the bloom of the pomegranate in full flush-

these awaken in my breast
a tremor of joy,
a tide upon the shores of youth.

Truly, thou art favoured by the hand of Providence,
and it is writ upon the noble union of thine brows.
Eyes dark as the forest deer's,
a countenance ever illumined by gentle mirth,
a character unsullied by the dust of dishonour,

a will firm and steadfast as the oaken beam-
these have ensnared my admiration,
and cast their quiet spell upon all
who are blessed to know thee.

The Unfading Love

Long have you stayed away, my love-
Yet never have I forgotten you.
You are etched within my soul,
An eternal song within my heart.

With you I wish to wander
Along the salt-kissed shores of the sea,
With you I long to play
Beneath the silver hush of moonlit skies.

Beloved- my only beloved-
You are carved in the depth of my being.
With you I shall sit
Upon the emerald slopes of the hills,
Where silence breathes like prayer.

I know, I could not return
The pure gift of your love.
Yet still you sought me,
Still you dreamed of me,
And in a mantle woven of love
You wrapped me tenderly to your heart.

Silent Resentment

You had said -
you feel it too.
I thought- perhaps you do,
but never quite as I do.

You came closer,
sat by my side.
Yet I stayed silent,
my pride refusing to let words flow.

Your anger burned,
my conscience bore its weight.

You had said -
you feel it too.
I thought- perhaps you do,
but never quite as I do.

Wounded pride kept me still,
stubborn silence held me back.
And why should I call?

For you wander in your own delight,
lost in the rhythm of your whims,
rejoicing in a world
where I remain unseen.

And then -
you smiled, a tender smile,
where pearls seemed to fall,
a smile that breathed new life,
a smile that swept away
every shadow, every gloom.

You had said -
you feel it too.
I thought- perhaps you do,
but never quite as I do.

The Enchanted Melody of the Forest

At the stillness of noon, a forest bird sings,
Its melody drifts on invisible wings.
Alone in my chamber, I press my ear,
Hoping its hidden message I might hear.
But what it sings - ah, I cannot tell,
The language of nature holds me in its spell.

At the doorway I stand, in silence deep,
Listening to secrets the bird seems to keep.
Is it telling of love, of sorrow, of skies?
Or whispering dreams that in silence arise?
I cannot decipher the words it conveys,
A mystery that lingers through the golden rays.

Why does it sing at the heart of the day?
Why does its music not fade away?
Perhaps it recalls some ancient lore,
A song of the woods, of life evermore.
Enchanted, I linger, bound by its call,
Yet I cannot grasp the meaning at all.

Oh, forest bird, sing your song again,
In your music lies joy, in your silence pain.
Though I may never know what you say,
Your voice will guide my soul on its way.

The Inevitable

When buds awaken, blossoms cannot stay,
If dawn is risen, so must come the day.
When clouds assemble, rains will surely fall,
Each sign of nature speaks, and speaks to all.

If winter whispers, spring is on its way,
If youth is blooming, passion will not stray.
When the moon is full, the earth must shine,
In silver floods, in radiance divine.

If man is born to walk upon the earth,
The stars will call him, daring his rebirth.
If bees have hives, then honey will appear,
If oceans beckon, jewels are always near.

For birth itself proclaims that death shall come,
The setting sun must end the rising one.
Thus every cycle, written, sealed, complete-
Life's timeless law no power can defeat.

The Bond of Relentless Love

You bound me fast with love's stern thread,
A chain of fire, by passion spread.
Wandering hearts, with envious eyes,
Gaze upon the truth they despise.
So I escape, yet cannot flee,
For every path returns to thee.

On rose's petals your face appears,
A timeless vision through fleeting years.
With you beside me, hand in hand,
I dream of walking on other lands -
To Mars, to stars, beyond the skies,
Carried by love that never dies.

I am Devdas, your Devda true,
And you, my Parul - eternally you.
Without your light, my soul is bare,
A desert wasteland, stripped and spare.

Yet with you, springtime's breath I keep,
Henna stains where our fingers meet.
Though winter's fog once kept me far,
Your warmth still shone, a guiding star.
At your soft touch, the frost took flight,
And dawn broke forth from endless night.

The Octogenarian

The octogenarian, companion of time,
Not faded, but glowing in wisdom's prime.
Through tears and laughter, his days are spun,
A sea of experience, histories won.

Wrinkles frame eyes that still shine bright,
Within his chest glows life's deep light.
Storms he has crossed with steadfast breath,
An anthem of honor, defying death.

His steps are slow, yet firm, yet true,
His blessings awaken hopes anew.
In his voice resounds a gentle song,
In his silence, lessons lifelong.

The octogenarian is life's pure gain,
Our sheltering shade through joy and pain.
To honor him is civilization's creed,
He is our banyan, our eternal steed.

Delight

I love the hilsa's golden taste,
if first through fire its flesh is graced.

I love the river's whispered side,
if grasses soft the banks provide.

I love to walk with hands in mine,
if touch be gentle, pure, divine.

I love the draught of lemon's light,
if sugar yield but soft and slight.

I love the moon in heaven's height,
if silence guards her tender night.

I love to wander, free, unknown,
if empty paths are mine alone.

I love to speak with the soul I hold dear,
if Time shall grant us an hour sincere.

The Aggressor

Never have I witnessed such desolation,
not in the chronicles of time,
not in the memory of any age.
What has the mighty gained from the meek?
What has the strong won by breaking the fragile?

They hunger to chain the earth,
to enslave its people,
to seize wealth,
to strip away dignity.
Aggression, empire - not inventions of today,
but ancient quarrels dressed in new armor.

Alas! The stranger's embrace seems warmer than a mother's -
they pose as guardians,
yet justice never springs from their hand.

And we -
a fractured, weary throng,
long schooled in obedience,
hearts still blooming
with fragile petals of hope.
They strike without warning,
upon our land, upon our flesh,
while we, weakened by unseen disease,
search in vain for a cure.

So the days erode.
Brotherhood decays from within,
its roots hollowed by worms,
while nations rise tall,
pretending their benevolence
is the pillar of our survival.

The Transformation of Taste

Old greens, old clothes, the meals of old days,
Fish in rich curry, in traditional ways.
Stews of vegetables, fried breads with spice,
Now give way to biryani, dosa, and rice.

The old native dishes no longer excite,
Without fast food - nothing feels right.
Burgers and sandwiches, sodas in line,
Western flavors the young define.

Taste has shifted, our roots left behind,
"Flavor" now rules where essence would guide.
Homeland forgotten, the foreign adored,
Our tongues march along a Western accord.

Hot chili sauces from lands overseas,
Stir-fried creations of far-off cuisines.
Slowly adapting, we mimic, we learn,
Losing the flavors for which we once yearned.

Royal rice platters, spiced meats divine,
Curries and sweets that once brightly shined.
Pickles and chutneys, skewers by flame,
Fiery yet heavenly- always the same.

Fish cooked with potatoes? Old rules said "no."
Banana with ginger? Tradition said so.
Yet fish with green papaya, catfish with green,
Simple, inventive- delicious, serene.

Food like ambrosia makes mouths overflow,
But too much salt makes the bile quickly grow.
Balanced with spices, measured with care,
Winter fish stews with herbs beyond compare.

Tender young neem leaves, fried crisp and light,
Bitter yet healing, a rare delight.
As poetry sings of beauties in nine,
Ayurveda honors six tastes divine.

Deliverance

O Lord,
Bestow Thy radiance upon my life,
Grant me the breath of true life,
Lift me from the twilight of shadows,
Deliver me from the mire of sin.

O Lord,
Kindle Thy light within my heart,
Make Thy meditation ever enchanting,
Cleanse my soul of stains and strife,
In dreams and in sleep, let me feel Thy fragrance.

O Lord,
Unfold my wisdom through Thy grace,
Awaken my body, my spirit, my soul,
Guide me upon the straight and simple path,
Spare me the sorrow of unspoken pain.

O Lord,
Bestow Thy peace within my soul,
Grant me strength in weakness, light when shadows fall.
In grief and peril, let Thy mercy stand near,
Through Thy grace, let my life bloom in eternal dawn.

O Lord,
Bestow Thy peace within my soul,
Grant me strength in weakness, light when shadows roll.
In grief and peril, let Thy mercy stand near,
Through Thy compassion, make my life holy and clear.

O Lord,
Bestow Thy peace within my soul,
Grant me strength in weakness, light when shadows roll.
In grief and peril, let Thy mercy stand near,
Through Thy grace, let my life bloom in eternal dawn.

The Thirsty Bird- *Chatak*

Your eyes are speaking, soft and true,
They whisper love from me to you.

Like chatak longs for drops of rain,
But clouds drift off to fields in vain.

This heart goes wild, it yearns, it flies,
It seeks your home, your soul, your eyes.

You drew me close, with love's embrace,
Your glance, your touch- no time can erase.
Your spirit calls, it pulls me near,
Your voice resounds, I always hear.

Though I may never walk your lane,
Nor sit beside your side again-

Still in my heart you bloom, you stay,
Through summer heat, through spring's soft day.

In lotus ponds, I see your face,
In shining hues, in tender grace.
My soul is full, my pain departs,
As seasons turn, you rule my heart.

Perversion

Degenerate arts, with poisoned grace,
Garish tales the mind debase.
Rushdie's ink, or Taslima's cry,
Serve but the feast where falsehoods lie.

Words unchaste, profane, obscene,
Portraits of lust on sordid screen.
Yet crowds delight in such decay,
Twisted hearts their hymns obey.

They court the blaze of fleeting light,
Barter truth for hollow might.
With conscience sold and honor slain,
They weave their fortune out of shame.

Unspeakable tales in crude disguise,
Adulterous lives they glorize.
In tempting debates their voices resound,
In twisted minds, their honors are found.

They yearn for the light of a fleeting fame,
Bartering souls in a reckless game.
Through shadows of falsehood they choose their way,
Selling their conscience for gold in a day.

A culture decayed, creations impure,
Tasteless allure the weak hearts endure.

The Unspoken Words

The words I hide, they ache, they burn,
Yet to the world, they can't return.
They weigh my chest, they cloud my air,
A hollow silence everywhere.

I keep them locked, though they implore,
For spoken truth would wound me more.
So pain must bloom, yet none can see,
The silent grief inside of me.

Oh, do not ask of yesteryears,
They drown in shadows, drenched in tears.
Behind the curtain, faint and dim,
They whisper songs of sorrow's hymn.

Unbidden still, they rise, they stay,
No strength can chase their ghosts away.
Though time may heal, it can't erase,
The secret scars I can't efface.

The Yearning of Tears

My wishes rest in streams of tears,
A restless heart flows with fears.
Like withered leaves in storm,
My desert-heart is bare, forlorn.

Hollow winds in my chest abide,
Each breath weighs heavy, none can hide.
What I seek, I sometimes gain,
Yet false pride binds Rāi in pain.

O silent night, conceal not the light,
Hope still glimmers in sorrow's sight.
From tears that fall, new blossoms rise,
Even in ruins, dawn paints the skies.

Though shadows weep and silence sings,
Love's flame sleeps beneath its wings.
When springtime calls with mercy's song,
Life awakes where tears belong.

Embrace

When autumn scents of *coral jasmine* fall,
And twilight whispers, soft and small,
Come, my friend, and gently stay,
I'll seat you warm in my heart's array.

If in some leisure you recall,
Come to me, come - my dearest of all.
And should the path bring sweat like rain,
I'd take it as dew, with tender refrain.

In memory's glow your face appears,
Unfaded by distance, untouched by years.
Your image shines though far you roam,
Its outline clear, a light in my home.

So come, my friend, with arms outspread,
An embrace awaits, as my soul has pled.
Each moment I wait, each breath is a prayer,
That you will come, and find me there.

The tablets of memory stand unbroken,
Your words still bloom, their truth unspoken.
Your presence lives, so vivid, so true,
As if each hour still carries you.

I know your work, your cares, your quest,
I'll never bind you - this I attest.
Yet in my heart you'll ever remain,
A cherished joy, beyond all chain.

By the Fields of Valley

By the golden fields of my valley,
Where the ripened paddy bends in song,
Farmers tread with steady footsteps,
Their shadows stretching faint and long.

The evening breeze adorns the valley,
Carrying scents of earth and rain,
Children chase the drifting fireflies,
Their laughter echoing o'er the plain.

But when July's restless storms awaken,
And the darkened skies with thunder pour,
Brother, I dare not walk the furrows -
Not then, upon that trembling floor.

For even the field of life is fragile,
When clouds of doubt and tempests near;
Without a faith, without a steadfast hand,
How can one harvest year to year?

Vanishing

I left my house, my walls, my humble home,
All for the love of the Prophet, Mustafa (pbuh) alone.

I gave the cows, the fish, the wealth I could spare,
And walked this world in solitude and care.
Human ways and manners left me confused,
In the face of change and trials, I felt misused.

Forty years of life have vanished in vain,
Counting every gain, only emptiness remains.
After all my striving, all my giving and pain,
I return reborn, in the humble guise of the meek again.

Those I gave for now call me a thief,
After decades of toil, I glimpse a dawn of relief.
Flesh and blood - humans will falter and err,
In life's third part, I reckon the dues I bear.

Blood binds us close, a world teeming within,
Yet blessings of effort bring only scorn and chagrin.
World and hereafter, all seem lost to me,
For kindness and patience, only blame do I see.

Alone I sit, pondering fate's cruel jest,
Mocked by the world, by none truly blessed.
Yet my heart trusts in Allah above,
In this life and the next, I shall rise by His love.
For only my Lord tests me, in His mercy and care,
Through every trial, His guidance is there.

Contact the Author

Thank you for reading ***"The Voice of Radiance".***
Your interest in this book means more than words can express.

If you'd like to connect, collaborate, or share your thoughts about the book, feel free to reach out through any of the following platforms:

Email: mamazzad.choudhury123@gmail.com
Facebook: Babu Choudhury

I welcome readers, students, journalists, and fellow storytellers to start a conversation.

Get Involved & Share Feedback
Share your thoughts on social media using hashtags like #TheVoiceOfRadiance | #LuminousJouneyOfHeart

Tag the Poet & Share Your Feedback
Whether it's a post, story, reel, or blog, your voice adds to heart, soul & nature's light.

We'd love your feedback!
Scan this QR code to share your thoughts on ***"The Voice of Radiance"***

Thank you for your support, your feedback enriches learning, upholds guidance, and carries forward the timeless journey of words.

Dear Reader

If you have reached this page, you have walked with me through light and shadow,
through words that sought to echo the heart and soul.
For this, I thank you -
for lending your time, your heart, and your quiet attention.

Every ending carries within it the spark of a new dawn.
If these poems have stirred a thought, awakened a memory,
or whispered a question within you, let it live on.

Poetry never truly ends.
In every verse I sought radiance,
in every silence I sought truth,
and in every reflection I sought the gentle touch of nature's light.

If even a single line has touched your spirit, preserved a memory,
or awakened reflection, then my task is complete.

Let remembrance rise, let reflection dwell,
and let these words echo -
not only in these pages,
but in the world beyond them.

With gratitude,
Mamazzad Ahmed Choudhury
Poet,
The Voice of Radiance

Printed at Repro India Ltd.